Tell the WHOLE Story

EMBRACE YOUR JOURNEY TO BECOME AMAZING ON PURPOSE

DAVITA GARFIELD

Tell the Whole Story

ISBN: 978-0-9979724-0-5

Book cover designed by Andre D. Benson, Abensonmedia, LLC

Back cover photo by John Allen Berry, John Allen Photography, LLC

For information contact :

Website: www.DaVitaGarfield.com

Email: empoWered4success@davitagarfield.com

Dedication

The women of "A Rose for A Rose" are a true testament of God's promise that when we are faithful and when we believe, He will make it happen. I believe God designed this group to touch us when we really needed it. Everyone in this group was placed by divine invitation, and I thank God for you all. It is because of this; I have been able to continue to walk boldly into the purpose I know God has for my life.

My company, empoWermentNOW, fulfills my desire to coach women into owning their role in taking the action steps to reach their goals. My women's empowerment group, "A Rose for A Rose" fulfills my desire for women to encourage, support, and at times, carry one another when our loads get too heavy. The combination of the two has inspired the completion of this book. I will forever acknowledge the women of "A Rose for A Rose" as the founding members of a movement that I am now purposed to share with the world. I am trusting God's promise to be able to reach and bless so many lives. I am extremely excited to carry you all with me on this journey as I tell my whole story and strive to be amazing on purpose.

Thank You

I would like to thank each and every one who loved, supported and prayed me through my surgery and recovery. Your support before, during and after that time in my life is what has motivated and inspired me to write this book.

Following the commands of God is not always an easy task. Authoring this book has come with a true test of faith and challenge in believing that I could get it done. I am always thankful for the many people who God allowed in my life right when I needed them — even if I didn't know they were needed. If I could list them all, it would take up all the pages in this book. But, I would like to thank two very special people for supporting me, pushing me, challenging me, double-teaming me and holding my hand through this entire writing process. Joyce and Andre, I know that God handpicked you to be in my life for a time such as this, and I thank you both from the bottom of my heart.

To the man who has always been a devout provider, my No. 1 supporter and my best friend, Dad. Thank you for always encouraging me to be free and open with my thoughts and life decisions, especially the hard ones. I also thank you for never missing an opportunity to congratulate and cheer me on through my accomplishments. Your example and influence in my life has helped to shape the woman I am today.

To Aniah Rose, God gave me a special blessing when He allowed me to be the mother of the most thoughtful, intelligent, kind-hearted and amazing person I know. You are my driving force and the reason I continue my journey to become amazing on purpose.

Lastly, to my dear Spencer — your death helped me learn how to live, and for that, my friend, I will forever be grateful.

Table of Contents

Foreword

I believe relationships are the new currency and only those that have them are truly wealthy. Unapologetically I can boast that I am a wealthy man. I had the privilege to connect with DaVita as a friend and work with her in more than one capacity. I can truly say, without words her presence speaks volumes. From the moment I met her I could hear her story in her smile. I could feel her passion in her hand shake and the whole room could see her light in her confidence. She is a billionaire of a woman, but the wealth of her wisdom and spirit is innumerable.

DaVita holds so many titles and wears them all well. She is a mother, speaker, entrepreneur, philanthropist and now an author of a soon to be bestselling and New York Times bestselling book. I had the chance to read "Tell the Whole Story" and was blown away. From cover to cover she uses her story and her pain as a GPS to purpose. I loved the book and I am certain you will too.

Marcus Y. Rosier
Transformational Speaker, Author and Communication Coach

The Back Story

What I have always known and continue to stand firmly on is that my experiences make me who I am today. They have contributed to my wisdom, my drive to overcome and my ability to succeed. They have also given me my passion for helping others and my acceptance as an assignment from God to be a transparent example of how to figure out this thing called life. Now, if only I could sum that up in a few steps, throw it in a book and change many lives. Yes, perhaps that could work, but if I am being honest with myself and with you, then I must admit that I am an everyday work-in-progress. I have failed my way miserably and struggled greatly through many of life's challenges due in part to my poor actions or no action at all. Even today, as I present this book to you, I don't always get it right. However, I believe in my heart that the true beauty of growth and helping others to grow is in the lessons we learn and share through our struggles, failures and successes.

With that said, I have been working on this book off and on for more than a year. I played around with the concept and changed it many times. My initial plan was to write a book that had a "fix your life now" feel to it. I planned to share a few of my experiences, sprinkle some self-help tips… and voilà! I would be done. Unfortunately, I struggled with using this format because it has been very difficult for me to sum up my experiences in a few short steps. I realized that it was likely because I had yet to create the blueprint to the perfect life, and I still haven't. This struggle contributed greatly to the delay and outright inability to complete this book for quite some time.

Once I gave the book a deadline for completion, I began to struggle even more with content. I was so busy trying to get the book done and show up for all of life's other obligations, including: working fulltime, being a mother, leading a ministry at church and sharing my God-given purpose with the world, that I hadn't realized I wasn't getting much of the book done. Although I had my book outlined with a scheduled writing structure, the content was not flowing at all. This led to frustration, which turned into the thought that I was incapable of writing a book and creating a block that I just couldn't figure out how to get around. This went on for several months and because I couldn't focus on the book, I continued to work on my dream and fill my calendar with activities and events that gave me the opportunity to share my message and work on my inner growth.

During my time of just "working" on me, I attended

the amazing, life-changing "Step Into Greatness Tour" hosted by Nehemiah Davis, award-wining author, entrepreneur and philanthropist. I found myself surrounded by many goal-driven people. I left the conference with several precious jewels to support my drive to go to the next level in my life. The first jewel I captured was from Marcus Y. Rosier, an author, speaker and entrepreneur. He talked about respecting your mind when writing or documenting your thoughts. Meaning, when thoughts or ideas enter your mind, it is your responsibility to stop and take action. To me, that also meant respecting and obeying God's instruction. From that, I realized I needed to move into action. Another jewel I was left with was from Kachelle Kelly, another speaker, author and entrepreneur who shared her response and obedience when God directed her to write her first book in seven days.

After the conference, I spent the next week in my quiet space and began praying to God for guidance on my next steps. At the time, I wasn't necessarily praying about the book, I just knew I needed to refocus on how to manifest my dreams into reality. After a week of continuous praying, I woke up one morning and started my planned routine of getting to work early so I could finish early. Without any warning, I heard the words, "Tell The Whole Story." I thank God for His grace because I continued to get ready until I heard the words two more times in my head before I realized what the words meant. I literally said out loud, "Ohhh, you meant for me to tell the whole story...duh!"

My "duhhh" moment with God suddenly allowed me to apply the two jewels I took away from the conference. I jumped right into action and began to write a new book. Now, here I had been struggling with writing this book for more than a year, and literally had 43 days left before my proposed deadline. I found myself starting all over with a new title, new concept and in need of a new book cover and promotional plan. This new energy and focus was a direct result of leaving myself open for God to remind me of my original assignment.

I have always been grateful for being able to share my story, and I believe that God tasked me with sharing my testimony of how my life has truly changed. It astonishes me how God will allow us to be in certain places, circumstances or situations and have people come into our lives that will validate or cause us to reevaluate our testimony. I know there is a group of people that I was given a testimony specifically for, yet for much of my life, I have not been sharing it. I believe my lack of sharing is exactly why I endured so many challenges and was unable to complete my first attempt at writing this book.

In less than a two-week span, I was tasked with speaking to a group of at-risk teens at a juvenile justice center and a group of women in a transitional housing facility. Although both of these speaking opportunities were scheduled more than a month in advance, I thought very little about the location of either facility. It just so happened that they were right across the street from one another. As I made my way to the first engagement, it occurred to me immediately that I was right around the corner from the house where I was raised and the neighborhood I spent most of my adult life avoiding. Walking from one side of the street where I parked to the side where the building was located, I was suddenly flooded with memories of the emotional pain I carried with me walking from home to school throughout my elementary and junior high school years. As if that wasn't enough, I repeated that same action less than two weeks later to the other engagement. The irony in the second building is that because of its multi-use, it has a front and back entrance. Although I entered in the back for my engagement, the front entrance sits directly across the street from the house where I grew up. I have not seen the inside of that house in more than 12 years; however, my mother still lives there today.

My time spent speaking to both groups as I encouraged them to overcome their challenges caused me to completely reevaluate my testimony, which became the concept for this book. I found myself engaging in conversation about my childhood experiences that I rarely shared with anyone. Although I did not expect these conversations to take place, my time spent sharing with both audiences encouraged me to think more and more about the importance of embracing my entire life's journey.

Can you imagine wanting to see a movie, and when you finally get the chance, you miss the first 15 minutes? By the end of the movie, you are really glad you saw it because it was everything you thought it would be and now you can't wait to talk about it with other people. But when you get around people who are having conversations about the movie, you begin to hear things being discussed that you didn't see. Now you are trying to figure out what you missed, but then you remember that you missed the first 15 minutes of the movie. While the parts you saw were awesome and amazing, clearly by the way people are talking, you missed some vital parts because you missed the beginning.

I finally had to acknowledge that not sharing my full story with those assigned to my purpose was equivalent to cutting out the first 15 minutes of a good movie. I have this awesome testimony and it is astounding that I was given the opportunity to change my life and completely regain my health physically and mentally. My testimony is so amazing that if you were not there when the change was happening, you would not even know just by looking at me today. But I realized there was still a part of my testimony; the first 15 minutes that was missing. For many years, I chose not to share this part of my life because it was my way of protecting myself from the potential exposure of what I considered to be embarrassing and degrading. I didn't view it as a testimony, but rather something very shameful that I fought to get through and convinced myself that no one needed to know about it. But God finally showed me that He had given me an entire movie, and I chose not to show it. It started with opening credits, music and a captivating opening plot, but I had chosen to cut out the first 15 minutes.

The lesson here was simple: If I am to walk in my purpose and help others do the same, then I have to be 100 percent transparent. I have to look back and map out the steps that I've taken on my journey to get where I am today and where I am destined yet to go. I have to "Tell the Whole Story."

Why is this book for you?

When was the last time you sat back and really examined and appreciated all that you have gone through in order to be the strong and amazing person you are today? If you have never done so or if it has been so long that you have forgotten the details, then this book is for you. Wherever you see yourself, it is important to understand that not taking the time to do the work and embrace the experiences that have made you who you are is likely the primary reason you feel stuck and unable move further in your journey to be your best you. This book will start you on your path of accepting, appreciating and continuing your journey to being the best version of you.

My goal for this book is to serve as a guide to help you accomplish four very key steps: Acknowledge, Accept, Release and Embrace.

- **Acknowledge** your experiences.
- **Accept** the role your experiences play in shaping who you are today.
- **Release** the guilt, shame or pain from your experiences.
- **Embrace** the journey as a whole to appreciate your greatness today and your greatness yet to come.

As I move through each step, I will share my personal experiences. With each step, I will provide a transparent look at the stumbling blocks that left me stagnant at different times in my life, my fight to get through those times and my work to face the fears of my past. I will show you my journey to becoming amazing on purpose!

Acknowledge

We have all had things happen in our lives that have shaped and helped to make us the people we are today. These things are called experiences. Sometimes they are good, sometimes bad and sometimes a combination of the two. We have all been faced with obstacles and challenges during our journey. It is what we do with those obstacles and challenges that determine the kind of life we live. Do we ignore them and just keep moving along? Do we focus on them and try to fix them? Or do we acknowledge that they've happened, but don't allow them to stand in the way of our personal growth? The answer varies for each one of us, and only you can decide how you allow your experiences to shape and affect your life.

Personally, I have been on the "yes" side of each of the three questions I posed. There have been times in my life that I made a clear decision to **ignore it** because I felt that if I made any other decision, I would have found myself stuck, unable to grow or move on. I call this my survival mode. It is a learned characteristic I received early in childhood, and despite my daily work, I still struggle with it at times. For me, **fixing it** came as a result of being in survival mode. When I have had to deal with new obstacles and challenges in my life, I often decide in my head that no one else is capable of helping me with these major situations. During these times, I will self-manage everything at any cost. At times, this has worked for me and at other times, it has completely worked against me. Often times, after much frustration of not being able to fix my circumstances, I have had to do the hardest work in my journey and face them head on.

As you read on about my experiences and solutions, please keep in mind that the purpose of this book is not to tell you all of the things I did right, but to encourage you to define your own "right" and do the work necessary to get as close to it as possible.

Chapter 1

IGNORE IT!

he ability to react to stress or trauma is dependent upon how well one can protect him or her self physically, mentally and emotionally. Blocking or ignoring the reaction to particular stressors can have various effects on the body as a whole. Have you ever been faced with a situation that caused so much internal conflict and discomfort that you chose to ignore it? If your answer is "yes," a likely natural response would be to choose to put the situation in the back of your mind or even out of your mind altogether so that you can move forward and/or not deal with it at all.

Learning to ignore experiences says a lot about who we are and why we operate the way we do. Exploring and acknowledging where this learned behavior of ignoring began can give us a better picture of how and why we react to many circumstances in our life.

At a very early age, I experienced my first life-changing challenge. Not only was I faced with the ugliness, pain and perversion of child molestation, I was also faced with not having the person that many of us would deem as our God-given protector to protect me from that experience. For many years, I chose to pretend that the molestation did not happen. I did a lot of work to tuck the details deep in the back of my memory.

For reasons still unknown to me today, I was sent to live with a family member that was not well known to me. During this time, I endured nine months of shame and exposure to inappropriate sexual activities, there by shattering my innocence at just six years old. It began with being shown graphic photos and movies of adults engaging in oral sex. I was told repeatedly that this was a normal way of showing love. Finally, I was convinced that I was to show this person love in the same manner in order to show gratitude for being taken care of daily.

I do not recall how much time passed before the first encounter following the initial exposure, nor can I remember how many times it occurred, but I know that it was frequent. I also knew from the start that it was wrong because I was constantly reminded that it was a secret and many people could get hurt if others knew.

While this repeatedly took place mostly at night or at times when no one else was around, I spent the rest of my time pretending as if it was not happening. I was a "normal" child who loved to read books in order to escape the real world and play "make believe" with friends to imagine a life that I did not live. I smiled, I laughed, I was polite, respectful and worked very hard not to reveal my secret in any way.

Eventually, I was returned home to my mother and family, and life as I previously knew it resumed. It was about a year after I returned that I believe I experienced my second, but even more damaging, emotionally traumatic event. While molestation stole my innocence at the age of six, the lack of protection from the very person whose womb protected me until the day I was born is what truly shattered my innocence. The day when the ugly truth was revealed about my experience is a more vivid memory than the continued sexual abuse I endured at the sick and demented hands of my family member.

I spent many years trying to erase the memory of being called downstairs and forced to stand up against the eggshell-colored, dingy wall with my head pointed down at the old grass-colored green carpet. It was right there that my mother demanded that I explain why I did not say something sooner. These demands were followed by clear instructions to never repeat this to anyone, ever. I don't recall how long this interaction lasted, nor do I remember very much about what happened after. I just know that when I was given permission to finally go back upstairs, a huge part of my heart, my dreams and my self-esteem — all in the shape of an 8-year old little girl — blended in with the stained wall. So began my hate for both her and the wall.

It wasn't long after that dreadful day that I chose to forget the whole thing ever happened. "Forgetting" was how I was able to get through life. I learned very early how to mask my pain and disappointment: first with smiles and then with lies. Later in my young life, I began to add makeup to cover up my un-pretty face and to hide the pain that was easily detectable in my eyes. For some time in my life, alcohol, drugs, promiscuity and bad relationship choices were also thrown in to mask the hurt and pain in an effort to forget the little girl that I had left on that wall many years prior.

Having endured the entire experience and overall violation repeatedly for nine months, and then being forced to pretend that it did not take place was how I learned to hide my pain and not speak out about anything that might be considered shameful or embarrassing. This was a regular practice for me throughout most of my life. I believe making the choice to just ignore it and pretend as if it didn't happen was what I needed to do to be able to move forward with my life at the time. However, years later, after going through the many steps of embracing my journey, I learned that my practice of "ignoring it" severely affected how I managed other stressors in my life that involved my relationships with others, work, career, and finally, my health.

What Does This Mean for You?

Sometimes just the mere thought of something that has affected us negatively causes us to not be open to doing the work to move forward. To determine if this type of reaction to negative experiences in your life applies to you, I would first suggest you consider the following three questions:

1. If you were to think about a specific experience in your life where you made the decision to ignore or pretend as if it did not take place, did that decision in any way manifest itself negatively throughout or in other ways in your life?

2. If so, how has it affected how you managed other experiences in your life?

3. What kind of feelings does this evoke for you?

As I continue through the stages of embracing my journey, I will share some key steps I took in order to acknowledge the experiences I originally chose to ignore, as well as describe the work I did to change how I allowed those experiences to impact my life.

Chapter 2

FIX IT!

ecause of my experiences, there have been times that I felt forced into protection mode when faced with new challenges. Even today, no matter what kind of obstacle that I am facing, I often feel that only I can fix it. I don't easily accept help from others or allow anyone to be a part of my pain for fear of embarrassment or of being looked at as being weak.

In this chapter, I want to talk about some of the ways in which I addressed fixing my own issues, as well as the effects that "fixing" things had on my journey to the person that I would become. As my life went on, I subconsciously harbored feelings of abandonment and a lack of protection. I became a master of ignoring anything that reminded me of my childhood. My rule for life was as follows: "I would do as I was told and I would act like it didn't happen. I would act like it didn't hurt me. I would act like I was not scarred by the things I was exposed to, the things I saw, the things I felt and the things I was forced to do. I would ignore the pain, frustration and embarrassment that I felt. I would go on with my life and I would become my own protector."

Becoming my own protector meant that only I could fix or manage circumstances in my life. One of the first situations that I "fixed" was erasing the physical detection of the insecure child who had become an insecure teenager. I learned very early how to put on makeup and put on a mask to become a pseudo-confident young lady who was perceived by others to really have it together. I always loved make up and how I felt when I made my whole face up. This was the perfect way to mask the little girl in me who never thought she was pretty. The little girl who could not have been pretty because if she were, all of those ugly things would never have happened. In my mind, if I were pretty, maybe I would have been hugged and kissed more, and maybe I would have been protected and nurtured the way every little girl dreams of. I never thought that I was as attractive as others, so I fixed it with the makeup. I would look in the mirror and see every flaw. It wasn't long before I could not stand the sight of my face without make up. Makeup allowed me to mask my pain and face the world. It gave me a false sense of confidence and allowed me to at least look like I had it "all together." This actually worked for me for some time.

My only issue with learning how to mask my pain

was that in order to have healthy relationships, the mask doesn't really work well. As I was trying to have healthy friendships and relationships, I was beginning to lose grip of my mask. I managed to get through college and other real life situations. Afterwards, I began to figure out what I needed to do in terms of my career, and started to shape what I wanted my life to look like. A short time after I started my career and purchased my first house, I stumbled through a relationship with someone who was also on his own path of figuring life out. Our relationship had its ups and many downs, but through it all, I experienced the amazing blessing of motherhood. I had been given the opportunity to love my little girl in the way that I always wanted to be loved, and be to her what I always wanted, needed and craved – a protector, a nurturer, a holder, a kisser…a mother.

At that point, I thought life was good. I had my career, I had my house, I had my baby girl and I had my makeup. Within just a few years, I was beginning to grow in my career, in my social networks and improve my family relationships. I was moving forward. When problems or tough circumstance came my way, I prided myself on being able to fix them. I was getting so good as the life "fixer" that I found myself helping other people fix their problems.

The natural progression of life seems to expose us to

more and more challenges and disappointments as we continue to try to figure life out. I can honestly say that I have had my fair share of highs with an equal amount of lows. To have had the opportunity to graduate college, begin a career in my field of study, attain a master's degree and move into a new phase of my career, which included middle and corporate management, are all extreme highs that I do not take for granted. I have been blessed to meet and build relationships with some amazing people. Many of whom I developed "family" type bonds with, and they support my journey to this day.

One huge low for me came when I began to feel like I could no longer fix the challenges in my life. In 2011, I lost my childhood friend to suicide. What started out as a summer crush 19 years prior when we met at an academic camp at 15 years old, turned into a life-long friendship. We had even gone with one another to senior prom because neither of us were dating anyone. Throughout the years, as we both settled into our own lives, there would be sporadic contact that went from months to sometimes almost a year before one of us would reach out to the other to check-in. In the few years prior to his death, we communicated and saw each other much more than years past. I have to admit that he initiated most of the contact.

The day I received the call that he had passed left me

in complete disbelief. It took another day before I had the courage to reach out to his family to confirm that I was not dreaming. I then spent the next month crying every day, openly talking about the pain I felt from this loss, and trying to understand why it happened. I constantly replayed the days leading up to his death, which felt like something out of a film. I was angry because it just didn't seem fair. I was angry that there were so many things going on in his life that he didn't tell me. I was even angry at his funeral because it was so surreal and unbelievable. I questioned if I was a good friend or what I could have done to be there for him. It had been a little more than a month before his death since I had last spoken to him, and the guilt was eating me alive. Had I known it would be the last time that I would hear his voice, would I have reached out more? Maybe I should have picked up on signs that he was suffering so bad with depression, especially because in hindsight, the signs were there. I replayed the sporadic phone calls at odd hours, including the nights I didn't pick up because I figured I would just talk to him the next day. I tried to erase the sound of his extremely sad baritone voice from my memory. I wanted to forget the many apologies for "interrupting" my life when he called because he was feeling down and just wanted to hear my voice. The questions and guilt-filled feelings were endless, and I felt like I was losing it.

I allowed myself just a little over a month to feel and go through all the stages of grief, anger and frustration. One night while having a conversation with my cousin who stopped by to check on me, which she did regularly, all I could do was cry. What would have normally been a visit full of nonstop laughter was filled with draining sadness. As she was leaving, she commented that she had never seen me this sad before and was concerned. I did not acknowledge at the time, but I translated her words to mean that she never saw me NOT have it all together, and I immediately equated that to a sign of weakness.

After that night, I did what I knew best and decided that in order to fix it, I would move on with my life and ignore my feelings. I would reapply my game face and show those in my world that I had it all together. I would stop publically crying or talking about it. I would put away his pictures and obituary and move on. This worked for a few months, but as time went on, it started to become harder for me to mask my pain and my ability to fix things was becoming more and more difficult. I didn't want to face the fact that my friend's death had changed my life forever. The more I tried to ignore how I felt, the more evident the changes were becoming internally and externally.

What started out as episodes of unexplained nervousness turned into full blown anxiety attacks at home, while out running errands and at work. I began to feel like I could not handle the everyday stress of life. I would get upset, be nervous or burst into tears because of the most minor things. I did my best to hide what I was feeling because that would mean removing my "mask". However, it wasn't long before the attacks began to get worse. My symptoms included an extremely fast heartbeat, shaky hands and feeling like the world was closing in on me.

I knew there was something wrong going on inside my body long before it showed physically. Day in, day out, I felt things changing. Yet, I still put on the mask. I had to keep it together. I couldn't bear the thought of having to explain something I didn't understand. So, I did what I had to do and I kept it inside. My levels of anxiety were building. Everything made me nervous. My emotions were out of control. The slightest things either angered me or made me cry. Most days, I was my "normal" strong self, but some days I just didn't feel strong at all. I felt weak. I felt lost. I felt like I was losing my mind. Despite the many good things going on in my life, I felt sad most of the time and then the physical pain started. I began to feel achy in different parts of my body and sometimes in every part of my body at the same time. I could not explain why my back, neck, legs, arms and head hurt for no apparent reason, so I hid it from the people in my life. On days that the pain was so bad that I couldn't even concentrate or think straight, I hid. I hid until the physical changes and the changes in my personality were so obvious that I could no longer avoid the stares and questions. Here I thought I had fixed the problem of getting over the pain I felt from my friend's death by "moving on," but in reality, I was creating a bigger problem. Because I decided that no one could help or understand, I closed myself off from receiving the help that was desperately needed in order to understand, accept and find a solution for the havoc my body was going through mentally, physically, emotionally and spiritually.

While it took me some time to finally face the reality that I was not doing a great job with "fixing" my circumstances, it wasn't until I almost completely lost control that I decided to do something different. I believe there are situations in our lives that we have the ability to fix and work through on our own; however, it is also very important to recognize when you need help and learn to be open to resources and assistance from others in order to get through our challenges in life. The key is to identify and seek help before things spiral out of your control and understand that it is OK to not be OK.

Questions to consider to determine if you are a "fixer":

1. When faced with your own challenges, how do you handle them? Are you likely to seek and accept help or do you do your best to try and manage the issues on your own?

2. How has that work for you?

3. Do you feel that you may need to re-evaluate?

4. If you find the need to re-evaluate, what would you change?

Chapter 3

FACE IT!

When faced with life's challenges, one of the bravest things you can do is face it head on. This can also be the most difficult thing to do as well. Facing a problem head on means recognizing the issue, and more importantly, acknowledging the need to make the necessary changes in order to resolve it.

As the episodes of anxiety began to increase with no relief, I finally had to acknowledge that I could not fix things on my own. After an attack that I did not see coming while at work, I finally made the decision to call my primary care physician. On my initial visit to her, she prescribed a medication for the relief of anxiety and suggested I see a therapist. At the time, I was still standing very strong in fix-it mode, so taking medication or seeing a therapist was not something I wanted to do. I knew that I needed to get the attacks under control; however, in my mind, I could do it on my own.

As time went on, managing things on my own was becoming more and more difficult. I finally decided to pursue therapy. Although I was reluctant to have someone help me fix my problems, I knew I had to do something before my mask was completely removed. Initially, when I went to therapy, my goal was to get a handle on the increasing anxiety attacks and to somehow get over the pain I was feeling due to my friend's death. However, not long into the sessions, more and more discussion began to take place about my childhood and the tucked away memories of the pain I felt during that time. It was during these sessions that I finally began to realize that the ways in which I had chosen to deal with my painful past were contributing to a lot of the problems I was currently having emotionally and physically.

Within a few months of starting therapy, my anxiety and depression worsened and I found myself back at the physician's office with a new diagnosis of hypertension that required medication to control. In the midst of this, other medical changes were starting to happen in my body that did not appear to be related at the time. My gynecologist treated me for endometriosis and Polycystic Ovary Syndrome. I was told these issues were the reasons for my bouts of excessive facial hair and irregular menstrual bleeding. My doctor started me on a regular birth control pill, and as a result, my menstrual cycle completely stopped.

Although I questioned him at every six-month visit, he continued to assure me that this was normal.

Around the beginning of 2013, I began to notice that I was consistently tired and drained without any major physical exertion. This was very unusual for me because prior to that, I had spent the last six years being a very active coed touch football player, a full-time mother and I also worked fulltime in a fast-paced sales and marketing environment. It was actually during my last season of football that I began to notice how exhausted I would be after just an hour or so of play. Back then, I had just decided that maybe age was kicking in, so I stopped playing around March of that year. However, the exhaustion continued. I began to notice that my skin bruised easily, took a very long time to heal and I had really severe bouts of acne all over my face and upper body area (shoulders and arms). I also had severe muscle and joint pain for no apparent reason.

In addition to the physical changes, my periods of depression increased and I could not explain why I felt sad most of the time. Despite the many great things going on in my life, I just could not seem to shake the sad feelings. It was around this time that I began to feel like I did not want to be around others, and sometimes, I cried daily for unknown reasons. My therapist suggested on several occasions that medication along with therapy could help with the depression.   The initial thought of having to turn to medication to help me through this time was absolutely not an option. I did not want to feel like I could not "fix" this on my own and medication surely meant that I would be considered weak and out of control. I adamantly refused to consider the use of any medicine, and the sadness continued. A few months later, after spending nearly two weeks crying daily, all while trying to hide it from my daughter, family and coworkers, I found myself lying on one of best friends' couch trying to explain why I could not stop crying. She gave me my time to be sad and then had a very candid conversation with me about her concerns. Her biggest concern was for my daughter, who had confided in her that she was worried about me because I was sad all the time and she didn't know what to do. Hearing those words broke my heart, yet I still had no idea what to do about it. Later that night, I lied in my bed still feeling bad and replaying my best friend's words in a loop in my head. I just felt tired of it all and wanted all the physical and emotional pain to end.

I will never fully understand why my friend chose to take his own life, but in that moment, I could imagine how he might have felt — so lost, tired and just wanting out. I wanted out. I wanted the pain and sadness to end. As these thoughts of "wanting out" entered my mind, I did the only thing I could think of to get rid of the thoughts. I stood up, got in the bed with my sleeping daughter and simply stared at her. I knew in that moment that not only did I need to live for her, I needed to do whatever I needed to do to feel better and ease her worrying mind.

The next day I reached out to a very good psychiatrist friend and began my discussion or antidepressant medication and how it might help me cope better. After having a very real conversation with her, I felt like it was finally time for me to acknowledge and face my problem directly. I started the medication shortly after. Surprisingly, I began to gain better control of my emotions. I felt like I could cope and deal with life's stressors a little better.

Unfortunately, the physical pain and changes I was experiencing weren't getting any better. So, back to my physician I went. I explained my symptoms to her and she had the lab to screen for lupus and thyroid function; all came back normal. I accepted the "normal" results for a few weeks, and then decided it was not resolved for me because I still didn't feel well. I reached out to her again and explained just that. She finally suggested I see a rheumatologist. On the first visit, he was great in taking my complete history, acknowledging and evaluating my presenting symptoms and then discussing his professional opinion and proposed plan. He ordered more labs to screen me again for lupus and rule out any signs of rheumatoid arthritis.   His recommendation and diagnosis was fibromyalgia. Although I had heard of fibromyalgia, I knew very little about it or how it applied to me.   This immediately sent me on my path of research, understanding and finally acceptance that this diagnosis "fit" me.   My rheumatologist then started me on anti-depressants that were indicated for the treatment and pain relief of fibromyalgia. For almost a year, he changed, added and took away meds in an effort to manage my pain.   Nothing seemed to control my episodes of severe pain "flare-ups," and the fatigue and exhaustion continued to increase. Although I was taking meds to help me sleep, I still wasn't sleeping at night due to the pain.   I spent my days completely exhausted, only to repeat the pattern day after day.

To add to my list of woes, in the beginning of 2014, I had a sudden weight gain of 40lbs in a six-month span. I felt like I just "blew up." My weight has always fluctuated, but I have always been able to get back on track with focus on my diet and exercise. But this time around, I could not get into a weight loss routine. I noticed that my excess weight sat around my stomach and breast area, but my extremities were normal looking. Also in comparing myself to pictures from just the year prior, I noticed that my face had completely rounded around my chin and neck area. I knew that I looked different, but could not figure out why.

During a visit with my rheumatologist in March 2014, I explained to him my desire to come off the medication and try a more holistic approach to managing my fibromyalgia – although I was already seeking "alternative" methods, like massage and natural herbs and supplements to support my body. He agreed that it made sense to come off the medicine if it wasn't helping. We decided on a slow wean process to better manage. Earlier that year, I also noticed a "fat hump" situated on the back of my neck, in between my shoulder blades. I attributed that to the fact that I had gained so much weight due to side effects of the various medications.

We started the wean process for the first medication and agreed to work on the second one by the next visit in two months. About a month before my next visit, I noticed that my episodes of severe sweating, regardless of the room temperature, were happening very frequently. This caused more havoc and pain on my body because I could not regulate my body temperature. During this time, I decided to cut my heavily locked hair that sat in the middle of my back because I felt it caused me even more neck, shoulder and back pain. It was then that the "fat hump" became increasingly noticeable. Not because it hurt, but because it was just so unattractive and my hair no longer covered it up. By the time I went back to the rheumatologist in July 2014 to discuss the new "sweating" symptom and the fact that I looked completely different because of the weight, he finally agreed to take me off the last medication and move towards trying a more holistic approach to manage my pain. I was totally fine with this, but just as I was getting ready to leave his office, I remembered that I wanted to ask him (or any medical professional) about the fat hump — primarily for cosmetic reasons. He looked at it and it was almost as if a light bulb came on in his head. Considering all of my symptoms previously pointing to fibromyalgia, he began to describe Cushing's Syndrome/Disease.

He explained that the "fat deposit" was often seen in people who had been exposed to steroids for long periods of time or whose bodies were producing high levels of the hormone cortisol. I knew that I had never been on steroids, so that ruled that out. He suggested I get my cortisol levels checked through a 24-hour urine collection and then proceed from there. I went home and began my research on

Cushing's. Almost immediately, I realized that this could be me considering that every associated symptom down to the physical makeup of a person with Cushing's fit me.

The next day I went to see my primary care doctor to address the concerns I had about my health, and more importantly, to share my feelings about the lack of support I was receiving. At the start of the visit, I asked her for 10 minutes to really go over everything I had experienced since I first presented in 2012. I believed from the time she started treating my varying symptoms, she had her doubts about my complaints and did very little to validate my concerns.

I am so thankful that I had finally made a decision to face my health problems, which resulted in me becoming a stronger advocate for my body as a whole. By the time I was finished, I think she finally started to believe that I was onto something with this potential Cushing's diagnosis. She connected me with the lab to start my urine cortisol testing and gave me the name of an endocrinologist to follow up with. After a week of waiting for my cortisol lab results and no luck scheduling an appointment with any endocrinologist sooner than two months, I reached back out to her for help because I was not willing to wait any longer. Finally, she received my lab result, which stated that my cortisol level was three times the normal level. She immediately reached out and found me an endocrinologist who would see me three days later.

My visit with the endocrinologist was very similar to my first visit with the rheumatologist. She documented all of my history and really listened to me as I described what the last two years had been like for me. She even asked to see pictures of me one to two years prior to that day. Once I finished, she discussed my lab results and told me that the level was concerning, but not enough to truly diagnose Cushing's. She explained the need for further labs and testing to validate such a diagnosis. She also explained that while she appreciated the fact that I had done my research and although I may have many of the associated symptoms of Cushing's, it was very rare and highly unlikely that I had it. In an extremely polite and professional manner, she attempted to ease my worries although I knew I had valid reasons for them. I went for blood work right after the visit and had labs drawn to test the cortisol and Adrenocorticotropic (ACTH) levels in my blood. Around 9 p.m. that night, I received an email from the endocrinologist with my labs results. Due to the extremely high levels for the cortisol and the ACTH, she was now highly suspicious that I may indeed have Cushing's. She wanted to get the results of additional 24-hour urine collections as well as a three-day saliva collection test to further confirm. Once these results were in, I was then scheduled for an MRI of my pituitary gland. Just two hours after I received the MRI, the tumor was confirmed. An hour after that, the neurosurgeon's office was calling me to schedule a pre-surgery consultation with the team of surgeons. In just a few short hours of learning of my tumor and confirming the reason for all the physical, mental and emotional changes, I was experiencing, my life was about to completely change directions.

One month after my diagnosis, I had surgery to remove the tumor. My surgery was successful and my cortisol levels dropped drastically. I spent five days in the hospital. I then went home to recover and begin the process of getting my life back on track.

Facing my health challenges allowed me to work through the problem the right way and use the proper resources needed to see positive results. My success with this approach left me with a better appreciation for taking the time to give myself the care I needed and deserved. Once I was ready to acknowledge my challenges from this perspective, I was able to outline the following steps to a healthier me. These are the step that I continue to follow today:

- Learn my body

- Own the fact that I am my own advocate

- Take action

- Do not take "No" for an answer

- Clear my mind and spirit of negative energy and people that could block me from seeing myself healthy

Journey Reflections...
Acknowledge

Suggestion:

Use this section to answer the questions in chapter 1 and 2.

_____

_____

_____

_____

_____

_____

_____

_____

_____

_____

_____

_____

_____

_____

_____

_____

_____

_____

_____

_____

_____

_____

_____

_____

An important key to embracing your entire journey is accepting the roles your experiences play in shaping who you are. Quite often, we don't understand nor do we spend a lot of time trying to figure out why we are the way we are. We all have specific reactions to certain circumstances, but we aren't always aware of how or why we react the way we do. These reactions are called "triggers."

When we are faced with experiences and circumstances that have caused us pain or trauma, our memory causes us to flashback to those memories when we are faced with similar experiences. These triggers could come in the form of a sound, sight, touch, smell or taste. A common response to triggers would to be avoid anything or any situation that could possibly cause an emotional flashback.

The ability to accept our journey is acknowledging that we do in fact have certain triggers, and understanding that they may be completely unique and personal. We must do the work to change our thinking and behavior when those triggers are negatively affecting us.

As I began to do the work to regain my health physically and emotionally, I had to begin to accept that I had developed methods for dealing or not dealing with certain situations in my life. There were times when my management of those triggers worked for **good,** and other times where I have been able to acknowledge **bad** management of my triggers and continued my daily work in my quest be my best me.

Chapter 4

ACCEPT THE BAD

In the very early stages of my work and journey to be my best me, I was tasked with journaling my thoughts, feelings and reaction to my life as it was happening. At the time, I hadn't done anything close to this in many years because on some level, I didn't believe my thoughts and feelings were even worth validating, not even by me. However, on 11/9/2012, I wrote the following in my journal about the little girl on the wall:

> *I hate her. I hate when she shows up because she ruins everything. Just when I think I have it all under control, here she comes messing up a good time. She is that homely, insecure little girl that never thought she was good enough. No matter how she dressed up or learned to cover herself in makeup to mask her pain, no matter how much you compliment her or tell her she is beautiful, she does*

*not think she is pretty or worthy of such
compliments. She is the reason I tend to hold
myself back from true confidence or feeling a true
sense of pride over my accomplishments. I really
hate her. I have always hated her. I hate that I
continue to equate my current feelings and
experiences to the characteristics that make up the
little girl on the wall.*

After some time and evaluation of why the memory
of the little girl on the wall was so vivid to me, and why she
reappeared in so many instances in my life, I realized my
trigger. That moment of being called downstairs at eight
years old to explain why I kept the secret of being molested,
and then being told that the solution to the problem was to
continue to keep the secret, was the very moment when I felt
the most unprotected. I was told that it would be "handled"
and somehow I knew in that moment that I was being told a
lie. And unfortunately, I was right. I was sent back upstairs
to face the rest of my life, trying to figure out how to protect
myself because clearly no one else would.

Many years later, when I was faced with trying to
manage the unexplained changes in body, this particular
trigger began to occur over and over again. At times, it was

coupled with yet another trigger from my childhood that I knew and recognized all too well. If you'll recall in Chapter 1, I described my experience living with the family member who molested me as a child. It was during this time I received the only spanking I ever had in my entire life. It came as a result of me sitting at the dining room table, crying in frustration over my homework, which was a rarity because I generally loved school and had very little problems. The unexpected shock of this spanking ended with me being sent upstairs to wash and change because I had urinated on myself as the spanking was taking place. I did not understand the impact of that encounter at the time; however, I do know that for the remainder of time that I was in his care, I never cried actual tears again. Not during the closely supervised infrequent phone conversations to the rest of my family. Not during the sexual abuse. Not during the humiliation I endured that included being forced to sit on the floor in the hallway with my back up against the wall and my legs spread wide in a pair of pajama pants that were ripped in the middle. I was being punished for ripping them. Not even when I collided with a schoolmate head-on resulting in the physical scar that resides in the middle of my left eyebrow. I believe that he ran into me and I ran into the corner of the wall as I was attempting to turn. I remember falling on my back and just lying there bleeding until I saw my teacher standing over top of me. I was taken to the ER where I received a huge needle to numb the area and seven stitches to close the wound. Yet, I never cried. Somehow, I immediately interpreted his response to my tears of frustration as a sign of weakness on my part. If I revealed how I was feeling, whether it be fear, hurt or lack of understanding, others would consider me weak.

These triggers have resulted in me spending many years of my life not wanting to appear weak or as if I could not handle "life." I consistently rejected offers of help from anyone because of my lack of trust and belief that the person was being genuine. My lack of trust, guarded feelings and believing that I would be considered weak led to years and years of bottling my emotions and trying to fix and manage every aspect of my life. There were times when I could barely get around physically, yet I would not accept help. I think about the many times my loved ones would ask if I was ok or if I needed anything. I would always say "no." Then I would find myself so frustrated because I felt alone and as if no one understood how I felt. I was in this never ending cycle of trying to figure it on my own and at the same time feeling defeated because I was on my own.

I did not know at the time that my life changing

moment was going to come at the height of my illness. The change came when I was finally able to face the person in the mirror I no longer recognized. Not only had my outer physical appearance changed that; this included hair loss, adult acne, gaining more than 40 pounds and easily bruised skin, but I didn't even recognize my inner self anymore. My personality went from being social and positive to being very withdrawn, depressed and negative.

I knew I needed to make a major adjustment in order to regain the life I saw quickly slipping away from me. I had to begin to see my life differently. I began to do the work to acknowledge and understand my triggers. I started to focus less on my current circumstances and more on my daily work to be my best me for others and myself. I began to take the time to stop and reevaluate my thoughts and actions as they were occurring and to make better decisions. I had to work daily to change the thoughts in my head by accepting my triggers as a part of my journey, and then making a conscious effort to change my reactions when faced with similar circumstances.

Chapter 5

ACCEPT THE GOOD

A major shift in my life occurred when I was able to accept my experiences as an opportunity to be a blessing to others. I believe that my experiences happened because there had to be a bigger plan than what I could see or understand. I finally began to get out of my own way. I decided to stop focusing on how good or bad I was feeling, and instead I began to use my pain, anger and frustration to help encourage others. On days that I felt my worse, I would seek to help someone else feel better. I finally realized that I had to take my mask off and be more transparent in how I was feeling so that others would feel comfortable removing their mask as well. My personal changes had amazingly developed into a movement that was way bigger than I had ever imagined.

The creation of my women's empowerment group, "A Rose for A Rose," started with the "selfish" pretense that focusing my energy on others would help make me feel better because it would allow me to take my mental and physical focus away from how bad I was feeling. The ultimate result was the beginning of a movement where women felt liberated by using their own experiences, wisdom and expertise to encourage other women through their challenges. Suddenly, I found myself surrounded by other women who recognized their own struggles, but also recognized that other women struggle just like them.

At the beginning of the 2014, I was having a conversation with one of my aunties, Denise Michelle Wooten-Troutman, about how I felt this call and desire to put myself in a position to help uplift, encourage and support other women. I had no idea how I wanted to do it, what I wanted to call it or what avenue to use to actually to do it. She told me to get a journal and write the following scripture in it:

Habakkuk 2:1-3

1. I will stand upon my watch, and set me upon the tower, and will watch to see what he will say unto me, and what I shall answer when I am reproved.

2. And the Lord answered me, and said, Write the vision, and make it plain upon tables, that he may run that readeth it.

3. For the vision is yet for an appointed time, but at the end

it shall speak, and not lie: though it tarry, wait for it;
because it will surely come, it will not tarry.

After leaving it on my nightstand for nearly a month, I was up during one of my many sleepless, pain-filled nights, and as I sat on the side of bed rubbing my shoulders in attempt to ease the pain, I began to think about how roses compared to women. I then started to write my analogy of a rose to a woman and how roses come in many beautiful colors; no one rose is the same; however, its beauty and pleasant smell is consistent among all roses. A rose represents all women. I thought about how we are all beautiful in our own different shades, sizes, ages, levels of education, occupations, socio-economic status, etc.

So often, we as women tend to fight hard to maintain the most pleasant view of ourselves, not only to the world, but especially to other women. However, many of those same women are also carrying hurt, pain, frustration and mistrust – past and present. Externally, we don't see that hurt because we are taught to mask it with our layered appearance. We are taught not to share the bad stuff because we don't want to be judged or viewed as anything less than what you see externally. We don't often accept or acknowledge the fact that the very experiences that caused the pain and bad stuff is what truly makes us beautiful.

Quite often we see, know, love, admire and even envy another woman because she looks like she has it all together in comparison to where we feel we are. It is very likely that she may feel the same about us. If we take the time to see past the external and share our experiences, we will likely find that just like us, she is not so "all together." From this experience, we learn that it is quite possible to help each other heal and get past our hurt if we just support one another.

I was so excited about my thoughts that I don't think I went back to sleep that night. I stayed up just thinking about the possibility of sharing my vision with the world. At the time, I was still very fearful of sharing it and fearful of being rejected because I was not in the habit of doing my daily work to be my best me.

Soon after I started putting my vision in the journal, I had actually tried to start a group on social media, but fear kept me from going through with it and adding anyone to the group. Now when I think back and considering how my life was on this path to change forever, I realized it wasn't fear at all. God knew I was not ready as this was during the time I was going through a series of trials and tribulations with my health, stress at work, the end of an unhealthy relationship and depression.

I had spent many "woe is me" nights feeling sorry for myself. There were days when I opened my eyes and before even getting out of the bed, I started to complain. Complain, because I went to bed in pain. I was up multiple times throughout the night because of pain and I woke up in pain. This had been my life for more days and nights than I wanted to count.

I finally had to shift my focus from my pain and sorrows and put a focused energy into helping others in their time of need for encouragement. This also meant I had to finally give my struggle to fight through all of these things by myself over to God. I had to humble myself enough to expose my flaws and show the world that I too was in need of support.

My daily routine of complaining had been immediately replaced with praying and thanking God for waking me up. I began to remember that my pain had a purpose. I struggled with feelings of shame and not wanting anyone to know that I was suffering for fear of being seen as "weak." That shame led to many nights of tears, no sleep and extreme frustration. Then I would wake up, put my game face on to go out and fool the world so no one would know about my true struggle. I spent so much time alone asking God, "Why me?" that I could not see or focus on the work I needed to do to change my situation. It wasn't until I changed my "Why me?" to "Why not me?" that God began to truly bless me. Dealing with chronic pain, stress, fatigue and a laundry list of other issues was a very a humbling experience for me. It forced me to slow down and accept that I don't have to do it all. I had to accept that exposing my "flaws" was not a sign of weakness and that yes, I do need help sometimes and it is OK to accept it when it is offered.

The women in the "A Rose for A Rose" have supported me at one of the lowest and most needed times in my life. When I couldn't sleep because of pain, when I felt depressed because I felt my life slipping away and when I faced the surgery to remove the tumor from my brain, my Roses were there. They prayed, commented, called and supported me. They showed me that they fully got the concept and my heart's desire. They showed me that women do want to support other women on purpose. They showed me that we do not live in a vacuum and that our experiences can help others. They showed me that sometimes when others offer help and commit to being there to support you, they mean it. They showed me that it was OK to be flawed and to not have it all together all the time. They showed me that no, we are not perfect, but we are perfectly imperfect and wonderfully made. We make mistakes and don't always do things the right way, but we can admit it, apologize if we need to and then dust ourselves off to continue on our path.

The most important thing I have learned and I am continuing to learn on this journey is that God has allowed me to go through this storm because He knew I could handle it. The blessings, love, support and open doors of opportunity to finally walk in my purpose are overflowing. God knows and now I know that the true purpose of my pain was not only for me to grow from this, but to also inspire and encourage others to accept their storms. The key is to fight through your storms and stay focused on God's promise to bring you out bigger and better!

Through daily feedback, participation and newly developed relationships in "A Rose for A Rose," I began to develop some common themes that many of us face. I put those themes in a daily context because our job to be our very best, is an everyday work in progress. Even if we don't always get it right, every new day we are blessed to see is another opportunity to do the work and to embrace our journey to become amazing on purpose.

When you believe that you are amazing on purpose, you can stop living your life with apology and lose the need to conform or minimize the person you are to please others.

Here are some keys steps that need to be taken in order to be your most successful you:

- Recognize and own who you are — good, bad, flawed and all.
- Recognize that there are things about you that require continued work every day.
- Acknowledge your work that is in progress and the purposeful steps to change it.

Free yourself and be open to the possibility that with work, focus and action, you can be amazing on purpose.

Chapter 6

WHEN THE PAST
MEETS THE PRESENT

One major breakthrough that I am grateful for is being able to accept the good and bad parts of my past experiences and use them to make better life decisions in the present. Having the opportunity to nurture and love my daughter the way I desired to be loved is a blessing that I do not take lightly. When I look at her, I see the most beautiful young lady in the world. In fact, the very first moment I laid eyes on her, I saw the same; although back then, I was afraid to say it. What mother doesn't think her child is the most beautiful child in the world?

I attempt to convey my feelings to my daughter as often as I can keep her hands away from her ears because at times, she doesn't want to hear what she doesn't believe is true. She believes I only feel that way because I am her mother and that she is the complete opposite. She doesn't see or feel what I see and that makes me really sad. I'm sad because she spends so much time putting herself down and pointing out her every flaw. I'm sad because in comparison to her friends, she feels that she is the least attractive and least cool. But what makes me saddest is that when we have these conversations, sometimes I get lost in her words and I begin to feel as if I am replaying my own thoughts and feelings that started when I was her age. Similar thoughts and feelings that continued through adulthood for me. I often think about the many years that I continued to tear myself down and mask my dislike for my "flaws" with makeup and smiles. This was my self-taught coping method that I used to get through my awkward pre-teen years, my "Who Am I?" teenage years, my "Unsure, but Faking it" 20s and into my "I Should Be Over This By Now" 30s. It took that long for me to finally begin the work to accept and love me to the core.

Now, the difference between my daughter and I is that I did not have *ME* for a mother. I did not have the opportunity to cover my own ears so that I would not hear how beautiful and intelligent and amazing I was. I did not have the opportunity to have that personal cheerleader rooting me on daily, no matter what I said or thought until my mind and view of myself changed. What I have come to realize is that while my experience and journey was designed just for me, it is because of all that I have learned and endured that I get the awesome opportunity to be a spectator and sometime influencer in my daughter's journey. I have vowed to use my influence to help her create and use healthier tools than the ones I taught myself. I want her to have complete ACCEPTANCE and love of self. Not with conceit, but with the self-confidence to know that she is beautiful and amazing in her own right.

I have often wondered why it seems that women can be so critical of themselves for so many reasons. My experiences have taught me that when mismanagement of challenges in one's journey happens very early on in life, it can be very difficult to correct. I know that this is a very crucial time for my daughter as she is feeling her way through the mandatory awkward rites of passage into womanhood. If she can love herself through this phase of insecurity, comparisons to her peers, physical body changes and downright confusion of self, then she will be ahead of the game when it's over. My continued daily work to be the best version of myself fuels my drive to help guide her journey.

Questions to consider:

1. Was your perception of yourself shaped, tainted or negatively affected as a young woman?

2. If "yes," what work have you done to overcome and change those perceptions?

Journey Reflections...
Accept

Suggestions:

Journal your thoughts on how you have accepted different experiences in your life.

_____

_____

_____

_____

_____

_____

_____

_____

_____

_____

_____

Another major component in moving forward is to release the guilt, shame or pain from our experiences. It is a common practice to base our personal growth on circumstances that are out of our control. We often forget that we are not responsible for everything we were born or placed into. Just as we did not get to choose our physical features, who are our parents were going to be, our race or the environment in which we were born, we also did not get to choose some of the circumstances we were exposed to that make up our overall life experiences. In order to position ourselves to release the hurt from these experiences, it is important to determine what circumstances we own and do not own. We must do the work to take negative energy out of our experiences so that they do not prevent us from moving forward.

Chapter 7

OWN IT?

My work to separate what I didn't own and what I owned about my experiences had to happen in order for me to begin to live my best life. For many years, I did not see the difference. As I continued to live in the guilt and shame of my childhood, I spent a lot of time feeling as if I had caused all of these unfortunate things to happen to me. I often felt that I created the space and environment to be sexually molested and mistreated. I believed that if I were prettier or if I were smarter, it would not have happened to me. I also believed that somehow I was the reason I did not receive the affection I wanted so bad from my mother my whole life. I never considered the fact that I was born to a young mother who may not have necessarily known how to nurture her children or effectively communicate with them. Nor did I take into consideration that she may have lacked these skills because of circumstances she was born into or exposed to that were not her choice.

Daily efforts to change my thoughts about my childhood experiences began with me clearly defining what I did NOT own. I do not own being molested, nor do I own my mother's reaction or lack thereof to it. I also do not own my immediate need to ignore and suppress my feeling behind the abuse. Once I clarified this, I had to stand firm in why I did not own these things. My reasons were simple. I was not given a choice in having these experiences. The experiences happened and they were out of my control. My next step was to clearly define what I did own. I believe that while circumstances and experiences happened without my choosing, how I chose to deal with them and allowed them to disrupt my growth is what I do own. I could either allow my circumstances to hold me back or push me forward.

I chose to take ownership over the many years that I ignored and masked my pain. I chose not to allow the experiences of my childhood to be repeated in my efforts to nurture, honor and protect my own daughter. I made the choice to break the generational curse of silence and not allow it continue with my own child. Lastly, I began to do the work to stop blaming myself for all of the difficulties I had dealing with the effects of the circumstances that I did not choose. I learned to accept myself as a work in progress at whatever point of the process I was in. As you move forward in your journey, be very clear about your plan to release the pain, guilt and shame from your experiences. You did not choose them. You didn't choose to be the child of an abuser or an alcoholic. You didn't choose to be born into poverty. You didn't choose to have a health condition. But you do get to choose how you deal with! It is important to identify what you own and remain confident about what you do not.

Chapter 8

POWER BACK!

T he interesting thing about our life experiences is that no matter how much we attempt to suppress them, they have a way of finding their way back into our lives at unexpected times. Mother's Day eight months after my surgery was one of those unexpected times. Prior to that day, I had only been in the presence of my abuser on two different occasions after the initial abuse I experienced as a child. When unexpectedly faced with his attendance at a family function when I was 18, I responded with a complete emotional meltdown unable to even be in the same space for the duration of the function. The next time I saw him was a little more than 10 years later at the funeral of my grandmother. I did my best to apply my classic "game face," ignored his attempt to address me and acted as if I did not notice him or the loving embraces he received from others who knew who and what he was. As time went on and I could no longer stomach being in his presence, I left the family repast very early.

Throughout the years, I would periodically replay that last encounter and I was disappointed because I could not even put my feelings into words. I allowed his monster-like presence to steal my words. I became withdrawn and unable to function normally. The anger I felt with myself for being so passive to the point of leaving the event all together stayed with me for many years. As time went on and I began to find my voice in other areas of my life, I began to stand up more for myself. However, the memories of the two encounters repeatedly replayed in my head. I often thought about what my reaction would be if I were to ever be in his presence again. I wondered if he would always be an unreachable, undefeatable monster waiting to steal my joy, my voice and my sense of self-worth forever.

Well on Sunday, May 10, 2015, on Mother's Day, I finally received my opportunity to face not one, but two monsters at the same time. My family decided to celebrate the birthday of my oldest aunt and matriarch of my family. Because this was a very monumental birthday, I planned to attend even if only for a little while. I had received a message from one of my family members that there was a chance that he would be there. I decided to go anyway. My daughter was with me and I assured her that we weren't staying long. I did my best to mentally prepare myself for a long overdue confrontation with my emotions, fear and self-esteem.

Upon entering the restaurant tightly holding my daughter's hand, I immediately noticed him standing next to my mother. This prompted me to walk straight past them and into the bathroom. As I was walking, I heard him ask my mother who I was upon which she answered him. **My initial thought was to walk back out of the bathroom and straight out the door. But as I looked down at the most beautiful, innocent, but confused eyes, I knew I needed to do something different.** I explained to her that there were some people who do bad things in the world and sometimes those people are in our own family. I assured her that I would be her protector and never let anything happen to her. I gave her instructions to not speak or look in the direction of anyone she did not know unless I told her it was OK. I explained that we would enter the space where our family was, greet my aunt and then leave.

As we walked back out into the main space, I made every attempt to walk through the room and directly to my Aunt. However, as I was walking with my daughter's hand clenched tightly in mine, he stood up and said, "Hello

DaVita," very loudly and boldly as if I owed him my attention. The "little girl" in me just wanted to run out the door, but the little girl looking up at me reminded me of all the hard work I had done to release the pain, anger and shame of my experiences in order to be my best for her. In that moment, I turned around and stood face-to-face with him. And just as confidently and boldly as he spoke to me, I replied, "I would advise you to not say one more word to me. You and everyone in here can pretend as if you didn't do anything to me, but I know what you did. It would be in your best interest to not even look in my direction from this point forward." In that moment, the image of the giant monster who so many years prior had manipulated me into participating in degrading and inappropriate sexual acts suddenly looked like a weak old man who had absolutely no power over my mind any longer. His only response was a weak, "OK," as he sat back down in front of his plate of food. I then turned to complete my task of greeting my Aunt, said my goodbyes to my family and proceeded to leave. The questions were coming from family members wondering why I was leaving, to which I replied that I would not stay where I wasn't comfortable and where the presence of a child molester was so openly accepted. Leaving his presence this time felt very different than the last encounter. I did not leave because I was angry with my family in any way. I left because I would not allow the work I had done throughout the years be in vain because the people involved failed to do their part in protecting me. I no longer looked to them for protection. If they could not defend me when I was helpless, how could I expect any source of protection now? Upon leaving, I felt this overwhelming sense of freedom. But, I still had to face my daughter who had many questions. I explained to her that sometimes bad things happen, and although no one did anything to protect me, I had to learn how to protect and surround myself with people who were capable of supporting me in ways I lacked as a child.

Her biggest question forced me to deal with the second "monster" in the restaurant. She asked me if I was angry with my mother for not protecting me. I was honest and told her that for many years, I was very angry and although I never treated her mean nor was I disrespectful toward her, I carried that anger around in my heart and allowed it to break me down emotionally and physically. I also admitted that I still had hurt feelings about the whole experience.

After that conversation with my daughter, I knew

that in order to truly release my past and take my power back, I had to find a way move past my 30-year-old hurt feelings. Dealing with this pain caused me a great deal of emotional turmoil and angst. I was suddenly flooded with memories I had worked so hard to tuck away. Memories like: my overall disappointment in the extremely minimal affection I received from my mother throughout my childhood all the way into adulthood, my decision to leave for college with a plan to never live at home again, the lack of phone calls or communication when I was away at college, and just the overall feeling that she was never really interested in my life. As I began to find my way into adulthood, my mother and I grew further and further apart. I made very few attempts to include her or seek her excitement or support about any new endeavors in my life. The long periods with no communication that spanned anywhere from a week to a few months became a normal pattern for us, and one day, I realized that it had been more than 10 years since I had seen the inside of her house.

The concealed pain that spanned from my childhood into young adulthood was now spilling over into fresh disappointments with our overall relationship, and I now realized that I needed to find a way to release that pain in order to move forward in my journey. It took about a week after the incident where I confronted my abuser, before I felt I could finally face the conversation. I called my mother and simply asked her why she felt the need to answer him about who I was when my daughter and I entered the restaurant. She had no answer. I told her that once again she did nothing to protect me and her protection was all I ever wanted from the time I was a little girl. Her reply was the same words she said to me when I asked her why she did not protect me after I had my meltdown at 18. She said, "I did not know what to do."

I knew in that moment that in order for me to be healthy and move on with my life, I had to release her from the desire I had to hear something different, to feel something different in her presence, to validate something that she simply could not validate. In that moment, she was no longer this monster who didn't love or protect her daughter. In that moment, she was simply who she was and I needed to find a way to get my validation, support, feelings and protection from someone else — myself.

Journey Reflections...
Release

Suggestion:

Use this section to list the items you own and those you do not.

_____

_____

_____

_____

_____

_____

_____

_____

_____

_____

_____

_____

_____

_____

_____

_____

_____

_____

_____

_____

_____

_____

Embrace

Embracing our entire journey is the final step to becoming amazing on purpose. The ability to embrace every one of your experiences is a necessary component to your complete existence. Every part of your story, positive or negative, has shaped you and continues to prepare you for your complete walk into greatness. Living your best life greatly depends on your ability to extract the lessons of adversity in order to face new challenges. Oftentimes, the adversity itself becomes the focus, making it difficult to see beyond it. It is important to learn from each and every experience and understand that it is not so much about the adversity, but how you react to it is what allows you to overcome. Finally, the steady work you do every day to become the best version of yourself is what allows you to fully embrace the journey.

Chapter 9

LEARN FROM IT

While on my quest to get a better handle on the unexplainable changes that were happening to my body, I came across a very interesting book that attempted to offer help on stress management. At the time, I definitely attributed my stress to many external factors, such as the demands in my new leadership role at work as well as my increased parenting role due to the out-of-state work schedule of my daughter's father. However, upon reading the book, the author strongly suggested looking at how and why the body reacts to stress in the way that it does. Specifically, how the body reacted to stress the very first time it was introduced. As traumatic events occur, physical or mental, our bodies tend to react in very specific ways, including the tightening or tensing up of our shoulders, grinding of our teeth or some other body tightening reaction.

The book suggested thinking back to the very first traumatic event ever experienced and recalling exactly how the body reacted. This suggestion immediately took me back to my childhood at the very moment when I was called down to be questioned about the sexual abuse. I distinctly remember standing with my hands down at my side and completely tightening up my shoulders. But I also remember trying not to show how tense I was for fear of being reprimanded even more. The "aha" moment in this memory came when I realized I would oftentimes carry my stress in my upper back in between my shoulder blades, even dating back to my pre-teen years. The book went further to suggest that how one physically reacts to his or her very first traumatic event becomes how their body always reacts whenever new trauma or emotional distress is introduced to the body. Over time, this builds and builds and ultimately leads to what many people call "being stressed out."

As I moved closer to finally figuring out the true source of my medical, mental and physical changes and knowing that all signs pointed towards Cushing's disease, I finally understood that everything I was feeling at 36 did not happen overnight. And it certainly didn't happen just because of the most recent stressful occurrence in my life. The overproduction of the natural hormone cortisol was a direct result of my body's mismanagement of stress my entire life. My initial and continued response was to tense my body, put my game face on and continue the status quo routine of my life. This may have worked for a period of time, but as more and more traumatic situations were introduced, the more of an internal beating my body took. This continued until finally the external lashings appeared. Understanding this is what allowed me to finally embrace that my battle with Cushing's disease was not an isolated incident in my life. Every experience along my entire journey is what finally led me to face this debilitating and potentially deadly disease. I needed to embrace all of the damage done, but more importantly, all of the work needed to fight for my life and start on the path to becoming amazing on purpose.

In my improved state of mental and physical health, I was finally able to reflect and embrace all the experiences in my life as part of my journey. I took the final step in truly forgiving myself and I committed to loving the whole me - past, present and future. One tangible effort I took in accomplishing this was to write a detailed love letter to myself that I read often. It reminds me of how far I have come and the work that continues to be done every day:

Dear DaVita,

I am writing this letter to let you know that I love you and I forgive you. I forgive you for all of the years you did not put YOU first. For all of the years you did not take the time to properly take care of you. I forgive you for spending way too much time being unhappy while trying to please and be accepted by others. I forgive you for carrying the guilt of your childhood for so long until you could see the physical effects of the guilt on your body. I forgive you for not seeing and appreciating your inner and outer beauty for so many years.

But I want you to know how proud I am that you have turned your life around and now see yourself as the humble, loving and amazing woman you are. I am proud of the voice you have found to advocate for yourself and for other women whose voices remain hidden. I love you for being determined to love your daughter the way you weren't loved as a child. I am proud of the example you have chosen to be for her and GOD. You are strong, intelligent, loving, thoughtful, productive, motivating, prayerful and amazing ON PURPOSE!!!!

Love,

DaVita

I cannot determine what the rest of my story will entail, nor can I avoid the possibility of new experiences that will be difficult to manage. However, I can and will continue to identify and use the tools necessary to be my very best.

Chapter 10

WORK ON IT

Our experiences make us who we are. They shape how we think, how we react and the decisions we tend to make on a daily basis to get through our lives. During this time, there are always going to be unexpected obstacles thrown our way that may attempt to deviate us from our plan. Things that change our reality with no notice at all. So often we are faced with trying to figure out exactly what to do and determine what path to take to get to the next stop in our journey.

In Chapter 5, *Accept the Good*, I mentioned the sharing of common themes that some of us face on a daily basis. The purpose of putting those themes in a daily context is simple. Our self-work requires everyday work and focus. Remember we are always a work in progress. The key is that even if we don't always get it right, every new day we are blessed to see is another opportunity to do what it takes to become amazing on purpose.

I wanted to close this book by sharing them with you, as well as a few examples of how I have personally applied them to my daily work.

Make It Happen Monday

"Making It Happen" is our daily work to accomplish the goals, tasks and dreams that we have for ourselves with the purpose of becoming the best versions of ourselves. Sometimes we find ourselves feeling stuck in our own heads because we feel as if we just aren't making any progress. It could be with anything — our jobs, completing a project at home, improving our financial status, following through on our goals and dreams, or even improving relationships with our significant others, children, parents, other family members, friends, etc. Making it happen is a daily job that requires clear steps to keep us on task:

Key steps to *Making It Happen*:

1. Identify your goals

2. Make a specific plan

3. Own your plan and identify the appropriate person in your life to help you with accountability

4. TAKE THE FIRST ACTION STEP in following your

plan

5. Stay consistent and watch *It Happen*.

Take Care of You Tuesday

"Take Care of You Tuesday" is a reminder that in our efforts to be everything to everyone, we cannot neglect our own personal needs. Oftentimes, we work so hard to be the best women, mothers, daughters, wives, colleagues, leaders to everyone who needs us, that we spend very little time being the best for ourselves. Some of the reminders that we share in the group include:

- I cannot show up for others, if I don't first show up for myself.
- My self-care (rest, retreat and de-stress) is a priority and absolutely necessary.
- If I need to say "No," I will do so without guilt or a need to justify my reasons.
- I cannot be the best version of myself if I don't take the time to prioritize my own self-care.
- When I take care of me, everyone around me benefits.

Through some very personal lessons and shared sentiments of the women in the group, the constant reminder to recognize the need for self-care has proved key in all of our journeys. An extremely helpful tool is to implement a self-care checklist to evaluate our physical, emotional and spiritual health:

- Am I eating properly?
- Am I getting enough rest?
- Am I emotionally drained?
- Am I surrounding myself with positive energy and people?
- Is my body getting enough physical exercise?
- Am I spiritually connected?
- Have I taken some time to relax and rejuvenate my body and mind?

Wisdom Wednesday

"Wisdom Wednesday" is a theme that celebrates the knowledge we have gained from the experiences of our own journeys. Sharing that wisdom with each other also creates a space to encourage other women and remind them that they too can make it through their challenges. The daily work in this theme is to use our personal experiences and passed down wisdom to remind us of how far we have already come in our journey to be our best. Many of the "Wisdom Wednesday" shares are coupled with inspirational quotes. Common themes we share include:

- *"Someday you will look back and understand why it all happened."*
- *"Laugh when you can, apologize when you should and let go of what you can't change."*
- *"You never know how one sentence of your life story could inspire someone to rewrite their own."*
- *"If we own the story, then we can write the ending."*
- *"Recognize and trust that what you are going through is preparing you for what you asked for."*
- *"Knowledge speaks, but wisdom listens."*

Throw It Out Thursday

"Throw it out Thursday" is the daily theme that forces us to do some self-inspection and identify all of the things that hold us back from being our very best. It then requires us to do the work to rid ourselves of whatever is holding us back.   Holding onto negative thoughts, insecurities, fears, anger and destructing habits, prevent us from making room for all of the work we are doing to **Acknowledge, Accept, Release** and **Embrace** our journey.

Below is a message I shared with the group recently:

> *When I was in the midst of my sickness and my body was changing, I spent a lot of time in*

"hiding." When I would take pictures or get forced into pictures, I would attempt to hide my body behind others or only take perfectly angled selfies so that I could hide what I did not like. As I look back on those pictures, I am reminded not only of the physical pain, but the mental pain I endured every day because I could not accept and love myself enough to not be ashamed of my appearance. Thankfully, through God, prayers, internal and external work, my body and mind was healed and restored.

I have spent the last year trusting God for the continued opportunity to use my testimony to inspire others to pray, love and work through their obstacles. In doing that, I have had the opportunity to stand in front of the camera multiple times and not be ashamed of what I saw. Lately, I have been feeling an internal shift in my body and my most recent photos are evidence that change is happening again. The old feelings of wanting to hide have immediately crept back in, making my daily work to love me no matter what is a little hard. But as I am a daily work in-progress, I will not allow anything that I am experiencing internally or externally

define me or keep me from the promise God has for
my life.

Today, I "Throw Out" the need to "look"
the part and to hide behind the perfect picture. I
will embrace and own my truth as it evolves and
changes. I know that it is all a part of my whole
story and my journey to be amazing on purpose.

Free Yourself Friday Theme:

The "Free Yourself Friday" theme is about releasing
ourselves from things holding us back from being our very
best...US!!!   I call it getting out of our own way and doing
the work to change our mindset. It wasn't until I woke up
and realized that I was holding me back from seeing my life
differently that I began to do something about it. During my
sickness, I had become accustomed to feeling bad and
feeling sorry or angry at myself for feeling bad.   It was
where I lived. I justified my right to not live life, to not be
present in my own mind and space, to avoid people and to
avoid facing the fact that I was sick and in need of change. I
literally felt trapped in my own body and I spent way too
much time justifying all of the mistakes that I made. I also
found myself justifying all the ways I had been mistreated
and made excuses for why I did not deserve to live any

differently. It wasn't until I made the conscious decision to change my thinking that I began to do the work to replace the negative thoughts with positive ones.

From this self-work, I developed the 8 Tips to a Healthy Mindset.

8 Tips to a Healthy Mindset:

1. **Choose to See Yourself Out of Your Current Circumstances:**

    Do not allow yourself to be consumed by your current circumstances. During the time of my health problems, there were moments when I felt trapped by my life. I could not see it any differently. The direction of my life did not change until I made the decision to transform my mind and imagine myself healthy — mentally, physically and emotionally.

2. **Replace the Negative Thoughts**

    Remove thoughts and words that say that you are not good enough, and you don't deserve to achieve a specific goal. Constantly remind yourself that you are good enough! Believe in the greatness in you. Believe that you deserve the promise that you know God has for your life.

3. Protect Your Space

Understand that you don't belong in every situation or environment. It is your right to protect your mind from anything that does not contribute to you being your very best. This decision comes with a price. You may have to completely remove yourself from certain environments, conversations or people all together.

4. Surround Yourself with Positivity

Our energy naturally attracts whatever we give off or surround ourselves with. If you are always around people who think and speak negatively, it is highly likely that you will also begin to do the same. The same goes for positive energy. It is a must-do step in order to begin to truly change your mindset.

5. Know and Respect your Limits

Don't allow yourself to be pulled into situations that you know will prevent you from being your healthiest. When you respect your limits, others will do the same.

6. Be your own Advocate

You are the only one who knows your body.

Stand strong in your right to advocate for yourself when it comes to your physical and mental health.

7. Enjoy and Embrace Your Journey:

Every experience you have – good or bad – was designed to be a part of your journey. Your ability to learn and grow from these experiences is what makes the journey worthwhile.

8. Share Your Story:

Your life experiences and knowledge gained have to be shared with others. Sharing your story not only frees you from the pain of your past, but it also allows others to be inspired to free themselves as well. It is the final step to a healthy mindset and to **Embracing Your Journey to Become Amazing on Purpose.**

Journey Reflections...
Embrace

Suggestions:

Write yourself a love or forgiveness letter.

Use this space to begin to tell your whole story and embrace your journey to become amazing on purpose.

_____

_____

_____

_____

_____

_____

_____

_____

_____

_____

About the Author

As a speaker, author and empowerment coach, DaVita credits the many life experiences and obstacles that she has overcome as the driving force behind her God-given assignment to support other women and encourage them to become amazing on purpose.

Saddled with an unexplained medical crisis in 2012, DaVita fought through stress, depression, frustration, and at times, anger to reclaim her health and renew her life. Vowing to never give up on herself, she wanted answers. Her tireless medical self-advocacy finally led to the diagnosis of a rare and life-threatening illness called Cushing's disease. After this diagnosis and the discovery of a tumor on her pituitary gland, DaVita's faith and determination to become healthy became even stronger. In 2014, the tumor was successfully removed and she remains in remission, good health, great spirits and extremely focused on living her best life on purpose.

During her time of recovery, DaVita decided to move forward with her goals of entrepreneurship and her passion to help other women do the same. She founded her company, **empoWermentNOW, LLC,** to provide empowerment and coaching support to women and help them to identify and reach their goals. Shortly after, she co-founded another business with her partner, Joyce Nichole Robinson, called #DreamsGoalsVision, LLC, a unique vision board workshop experience designed to help women create their vision for life, make a plan to reach their goals and take action to make it all happen.

DaVita's No. 1 role is being a mother to her amazing 12-year-old daughter, Aniah Rose. DaVita holds a bachelor's degree in social work and a master's degree in health administration. She has more than 15 years of experience helping people in the healthcare field, including her current role as a corporate director of marketing for a number of skilled nursing facilities. She also serves as ministry leader for the multi-media ministry at her church, where she feeds her passion to serve God and uses her marketing skills through the use of multiple media outlets such as audio, video and social media.

Presently, DaVita has expanded her brand and services into some amazing programs, all in the spirit of helping others reach their highest level of success without apology.

Stay Connected with DaVita

Website: www.DaVitaGarfield.com

Email: empoWered4success@davitagarfield.com

Facebook: EmpowermentNOWDaVitaGarfield

Twitter: @DaVitaGarfield

Instagram: @davita_empowermentnow